Berlin/Wall

David Hare was born in Sussex in 1947 and is now one of Britain's most internationally performed playwrights. Fourteen of his plays have been presented at the National Theatre, including *Plenty*, *The Secret Rapture*, *Skylight*, *Amy's View*, *Stuff Happens*, *Gethsemane* and a trilogy about the Church, the Law and the Labour Party – *Racing Demon*, *Murmuring Judges* and *The Absence of War*. He performed in his own first play about Israel and Palestine, *Via Dolorosa*, both in the West End and on Broadway. He has written the screenplays for many feature films, recently including *The Hours* and *The Reader*.

DAVID HARE

Berlin / Wall

Two Readings

ff

faber and faber

First published in Great Britain in 2009
by Faber and Faber Limited
74–77 Great Russell Street, London WC1B 3DA

Typeset by Country Setting, Kingsdown, Kent CT14 8ES
Printed in England by CPI Bookmarque, Croydon, Surrey

A CIP record for this book
is available from the British Library

ISBN 978–0–571–25130–8

2 4 6 8 10 9 7 5 3

For Stephen

Contents

Berlin, read by the author, received its first performance in the Lyttelton auditorium of the National Theatre, London, on 10 February 2009. The director was Stephen Daldry, with lighting by Rick Fisher.

Wall, read by the author, received its first performance at the Royal Court Theatre, London, on 12 March 2009. The director was Stephen Daldry.

The plays were first performed together as part of the HighTide Festival at Snape Maltings in May 2009.

BERLIN

'Berlin is the testicles of the West.
Every time I want to make the West scream,
I squeeze on Berlin.'

Nikita Khrushchev

Here I am, I'm back in Berlin, and as usual I can't get the hang of it.

I've been coming to this city, off and on, for well over thirty years and each time it's different. The world has changed and so has Berlin. In the mid-1970s, I was booed in the Schiller Theater, which today I can't even find. One afternoon, I remember watching Samuel Beckett instructing a couple of German actors in what looked like an over-directed production of *Waiting for Godot*. Beckett was holding a notebook and calling out moves which the actors had to follow. The notebook was later published in facsimile, as though it were a sacred document, complete with the little footmarks you used to see at the Arthur Murray School of Dancing.

And in the evening I was booed.

You have to understand the convention. If a playwright is known to be in a German city for a first night, he or she has to take a curtain call. To remain in your seat, to fail to go up on the stage is to imply disownership of the production. That night, after watching Beckett pad up and down the stalls, I saw one of my own plays, in a monumental decor by someone who had obviously never been to England. One scene was set on Guildford railway station. The platform sign saying 'Guildford' was painted in huge Gothic lettering which didn't immediately evoke British Railways. The vaulted waiting room was panelled entirely in mahogany. Like Kafka's America, this was a country of the imagination. Some youths in leather were playing on the Guildford station pin-ball machine, while drinking schnapps.

Oh yes, Berlin's a strange city. Hitler, then Stalin.

It's one of those cities which people say is very alive, yet when I look I can't see anything moving. Is it me? People tell you all the time that it's very young, but in my hotel everyone seems to be pulling their suitcases round on wheels and getting out at the wrong floor. Also, the arts are thriving. Why do you love Berlin, I ask when people say 'I *love* Berlin'? 'Oh, the arts,' they say. 'And the clubs. It's a great city for clubbing.'

So here I am once more, missing the point. Or perhaps not able to find it. 'Berlin is the most exciting city in Europe.' 'David, you should really buy an apartment in Kreuzburg.' 'Should I? Goodness. Why?' 'Everyone's buying apartments in Kreuzburg. It's a great time to buy. It's the most fashionable area.' 'Where exactly is Kreuzberg?' I ask. The inevitable answer: 'You're in it.' 'Really? This is the most fashionable area? *This*?' And why would I buy an apartment in Berlin, anyway? Where would I be on my way to when I visited my apartment? And hold on a sec, I thought I was in Charlottenburg. They seem to have moved Charlottenburg since yesterday. Every morning I'm driven from the hotel which we can all agree is just off Kurfürstendamm, and we seem to take a different direction. Or rather, more subtly, each of the innumerable suburbs seems to be rebuilt daily in a different place.

Berlin is harder than it used to be because the most famous landmark has gone. 'You're in the East,' my driver keeps saying, in spite of the fact he himself is barely old enough to remember the Wall. Then later: 'You're in the West.' But the dedicated tourists who go looking for Berlin's distinguishing feature can't find it. They made a big mistake. They pulled it down. In fact I just read a piece in the paper saying for the forthcoming celebrations they're planning to project a hologram of the Wall, to get over the inconvenient fact it isn't there.

It's not that nostalgia for communism is widespread – it's there, yes, but it's confined to a certain generation, to the memory of universal childcare, jobs, to the little shops selling memorabilia – plates and cups and teaspoons of the ideology. No, you see, much more important, it's bad marketing: the city of the famous Wall not actually having a wall. And the argument about the Wall is one part of a much larger argument the city has been having with itself, what it calls the *Haupstadtdebatte*. What do we do about the capital? What do we do about the past?

Ah yes. The past.

I keep thinking I'm going to put a line in a play. The line is: As you get old, memory does the work of fantasy. I never do, I never use the line, mainly because I don't care for those playwrights – Joe Orton is one offender, Enid Bagnold is another – who keep their fridges crammed with cracking lines, which nobody ever said, and bring them out when the audience feels peckish. 'Here's one I prepared earlier.' I find epigrammatic playwriting depressing. Yet I would love to get this particular sentiment in a play: When you're young, you fantasise about the future. When you're old you fantasise about the past.

That's why every time I pass the Zoo Palast I get a curious sensation. For me, Berlin is always cold. I've never been colder than when I served on the jury of the Berlin Film Festival. It was towards the end of the last century. Our hotel was six hundred yards from the cinema, and it was minus twenty. We had to watch three films a day – so we went back and forth, back and forth in the driving snow, each time walking past the zoo and

5

wondering how the poor animals were coping. At least they were still alive. In 1945, the citizens of Berlin, for want of anything else, ate the entire zoo.

The chairman of the jury was a French politician. At the judging it wasn't hard to predict his taste. 'Can't we give Catherine Deneuve a life-time award?' He despised *The English Patient*, which he said was vulgar Hollywood trash, with no redeeming features – except, perhaps, for the performance of Juliette Binoche. I said, 'Jacques, there's only one way you'd give that film an award. If they retitled it *The French Patient*.' The director of the festival said he was pleased to have got me and Jacques on the same jury, since Jacques was currently the French Minister of Culture. His English friends had told him that I was going to be the British Minister of Culture in the incoming Blair government. I told him perhaps he should look for new friends.

So whenever I'm in Berlin I have this weird feeling that, whatever the weather, it's cold underneath. This week when I arrived at Tegel, the sun was a surprise. It's never certain you're going to land at Tegel because this city of three and a half million people has three airports already and is planning a fourth. My favourite is Tempelhof. I love flying from Tempelhof. In fact, if Tempelhof took you anywhere but Belgium, I'd use it all the time. The terminal is the largest building in Berlin. It's a mile long and it looks like a fascist railway station. Never has so much authoritarian space served so few. You walk the full length of its enormous brown concourse, to arrive at one little stand: 'Brussels Airways'. When you walk to the tiny city-hopper, you feel like a character in *Casablanca*.

The Luftwaffe flew out of here, and this is the airfield of the Berlin airlift. Between June 1948 and May 1949, allied squadrons landed a C-47 or a DC-4 every ninety seconds to break the Soviet blockade, delivering two millions tons of food and fuel to a city so much nearer to Poland than it is to the Rhine. Today the field is a vast, eerie expanse of empty scrub. They're having a city-wide referendum to decide its fate – should it be preserved, an arena of living history, or should it be swept away, like the wall? *Haupstadtdebatte.* Everyone in Berlin will vote. But people keep pointing out, as if it were obvious, that the result of the referendum won't be binding. What's the point then, I say, what's the point of a referendum? Anyway, they say, it isn't just an airport, it's a club. *It's a club?* Yes, for transvestites. *Tempelhof's a club? For transvestites?* Is this city completely insane? Is the Reichstag a club? Is the Jewish Museum a club?

'It's a city for the young, it's a city for clubbing.' Jesus Christ, how many more times? Have I been to the Kit-Kat Club? No I don't think so. Is that the one where they fry poo in the basement? No, I think I'd remember if I'd been there. 'What are you doing here?' 'Well actually I'm writing a film.' 'What about?' 'Post-war German guilt.' 'Oh. OK.' Like that's the reaction, because one of the things about the people here is that they're so nice. And be clear, I'm not one of those over-sophisticated people who thinks niceness is just a mask. I think niceness is not a mask. I think it's niceness and I'm grateful for it wherever I find it.

Because the young Germans are so polite, nobody asks what I would ask, which is 'What does an Englishman think he's doing writing about German guilt?' An obvious question, you might think, but one which so far has never been put. Given that my prime minister was once Winston Churchill, the man who said, 'The Germans should be made to suffer in their homelands and cities, let them have a good dose where it will hurt them most,' you might expect just a trace of a resentment towards an itinerant screenwriter, blowing into town. For the German screenwriters' union, 'Leave post-war German guilt to the Germans' would be a fair banner to march under.

But the days of marching are over. The days of brown shirts and then of red flags.

I meant to say, by the way, about the booing – I rather liked it. I didn't mind it at all. Of course I would prefer to have been cheered – I'm not an idiot – but given that they didn't like what I'd written – no, let's be honest, they thought that what I'd written was *not good* – that being the shared assumption of what sounded like the whole audience, then booing wasn't bad. You could get used to it. In fact, I did get used to it. I came back the following year and was booed for a different play. Eventually, I got booed all over Germany. I'd say to my agent, 'I'm going to Hamburg tomorrow to be booed.'

There was something quite refreshing in standing there, like King Lear, inviting the storm, as if something covert were for once being made explicit. Both sides were travelling to something truthful, the audience liberated to say what they're always secretly thinking: 'You bastard, you've wasted my evening.' And me standing there, proud, defiant – 'Yes, it's me. I'm the man who wasted your evening.' I enjoyed it, giving physical presence to the old 'fuck off' which is the mark of all good playwriting. And bad playwriting, too, unfortunately.

This time, I'm less exposed. This time, I'm lurking in the credits. I'm here because I've adapted Bernhard Schlink's novel *The Reader*. Most literature of the Holocaust is from the point of view of its victims. *The Reader* is from the point of view of the perpetrators, and the succeeding generation. That's one of the reasons why it's so popular – in Germany everyone reads it at school – but it's also controversial. Some people don't think that the Germans are entitled to a point of view, and, even if they are, there are plenty of people who really don't want to hear it. Who can blame them? I keep remembering the Jewish philosopher Theodor Adorno who, one day, was listening to a speech by a professional historian of the Holocaust, Elie Wiesel. Adorno was both attracted and repelled by Wiesel's passion. He turned to a friend and said, 'Anything you can say about the concentration camps is at the same time both too much and not enough.'

'Too much and not enough.' 'Too much and not enough.' That's what I keep muttering whenever I'm here. Who can be honest? And what would it mean to be honest? I certainly don't think the French are honest. I was in Paris, by chance, in 1994, on the fiftieth anniversary of what only the French call the Battle of Paris. President Chirac organised a huge parade down the Champs-Elysées. The real survivors of the French resistance refused to take part, on the grounds that they didn't recognise anyone who was now claiming to have resisted. Their countrymen had told themselves so many lies about collaboration – not least in order to seize ownership of resistance from the communists – that any commemorative event was nothing more than a celebration of dishonesty.

But are the British any better? 'The good war.' 'The just war.' Oh yes? If that's what it was, why do we have to pretend it was fought without cost? Endless films with Richard Todd and John Mills and Kenneth More achieving a purely domestic stardom by stiffening their lips and muttering 'Hello, old girl' when reunited with their dogs or with their women. The lower orders confined to chipping in with a cheery salute and 'Permission to win the war, sir?' You wouldn't know from British cinema that seventy-eight per cent of European Jews were deliberately murdered. Or that, in all, seventy-two million people died in that particular engagement. Is it only the Brits who like to pretend that there can be such a thing as a war which is moving without being upsetting?

I'm stirred up, but is anyone else? Look at the everyday surface of Berlin, quotidian Berlin, once the city of confrontation, the city of demarcation, one ideology divided against another and separated by a wall. What was Hitler's ambition? To conquer Europe, certainly, but only as a pastime while he pursued his two more serious purposes: to kill the Jews and to rebuild Berlin. Read Speer. Why was Speer favoured? Why were Speer and Hitler intertwined? Speer found himself as close as anyone ever got to the great dictator. Because Albert Speer was what Adolf Hitler dreamed of being.

He was an architect.

Hitler pored over the plans, day and night, wasting his valuable time on the building-over of a radical city which had always hated him, which represented decadence, scepticism and dissent. And I do mean build over.

Well, now as I drive round the Haupstadt – no, correction, as I'm driven round – I see Hitler got what he wanted: not only was pre-war Berlin destroyed by allied bombardment, but key parts of what was once Soviet Berlin have vanished as well, torn down in the last twenty years in a fit of righteous horror at past sufferings. In 1989, it was predicted that the reunification of Berlin would present the greatest architectural opportunity of the century. But truthfully, how has it worked out? Apart from Norman Foster's rubber johnny on the old Reichstag, and some cute Toledo-blade buildings by Renzo Piano on Potsdamer Platz, what is there of real distinction?

Certainly nobody thinks much of the new American Embassy, the product of years of unpleasant negotiation and finally dumped down in the middle of Pariser Platz. It's already nicknamed Fort Knox at the Brandenburg

Gate. What do the Americans intend? Are they setting out to offend? They say no, for them it's a piece of deliberate symbolism, to build their embassy where the Wall once ran. Freedom, at last, arriving where there was none before. But if that's the intention, why is the embassy such an undistinguished lump of Cold War blah, a post-9/11 bunker of over-reach and paranoia, a supposedly secure building screaming 'We're insecure!' The *Frankfurter Allgemeine* has a pointed question: Will the embassy be besieged by tourists asking the way to the waterboarding area?

Admittedly, there is the famous Memorial to the Murdered Jews of Europe, over which views are much more evenly divided. What other nation, asks the novelist Martin Walser, as if his patience were finally snapping after sixty years, feels the need to memorialise its own disgrace? 2,711 identical concrete slabs are laid out over an area of 204,400 square feet. A decision was made and approved: no text, no images. Why not? Because anything the architect might want to say, any decoration he might wish to add would be – hey! What was it Adorno said? – 'Too much and not enough.'

'I like to think people will use it for short cuts,' said the architect Peter Eisenman when the Memorial was opened in 2005. At the start he'd even encouraged people to leave graffiti on the bare stones, slow, it seems, to realise just what the graffiti was likely to be. But the chemical agent he then used to make the Memorial graffiti-proof turned out to be made by a company called Degussa, which was part of a group with another company called Degesch, who had, in their time, manufactured the gas Zyklon B.

Oh yes, it's the usual human mess. Hard to disentangle the past, isn't it? Do you find that?'The right intentions? The wrong result?

In that sense, Berlin's a truer city than most, truer because it's a city without set pieces. Where are the great views? The great vistas? What hill can you climb and see it all? One afternoon, I drive the broad highway of Unter der Linden, down which Napoleon once rode his army. I'm here to sit with Gerhard Werle, who's advising on legal aspects of the film. He's Professor of International Law and Legal History at Humboldt University. His address is 6 Unter den Linden. Gerhard is the man you go to if you want to know whether your war is going to be legal or not. He's as clever as anyone I've ever met. How do I know he's clever? Gerhard does this thing only really clever people do. He listens to your questions, and then he answers 'Yes' or 'No'. Sometimes he goes further. He says 'I don't know'. Gerhard doesn't vomit words over you. He doesn't need to prove he knows more than you do. 'Yes.' 'Maybe.' 'Let me think.' As he answers my questions about the Auschwitz trial in the early sixties, I look out of the windows onto the courtyard outside. Some students in denim are staring down at what looks like a paving stone. No, it's not a paving stone, it's a glass disc, set into the ground. Ah yes, of course.

So that's where the Nazis burnt the books.

It's so typical, I keep saying to myself, this is my fault, I'm not doing this right. I don't like this feeling of being thick. It may be because of the work I'm doing. Screenwriting's a weird undertaking at the best of times, a test of character. Briefly you're in control, then for so much longer you're not. Especially when you're adapting someone else's work. 'In the book . . .' the actors keep saying, holding up the book. 'Yes I know,' I say. 'I changed it.' 'Why did you change it?' 'Hell, I don't know. *For the common good?* Films and books are different things. They work differently.' 'Yes, but don't you think this scene's much better in the book?' 'No, I don't, or else I'd have just copied it out. See how you'd have liked that.'

12

You see, the actors love it, of course they do, and why not? They have two sources of inspiration. On one side, look, the original book, full of words and thoughts which would take approximately thirty-eight hours to read out loud. And on the other, there, look, my little script which seeks, without anyone noticing, to digest those thoughts and words and give them some hidden shape and flow. The actors keep wanting to take bits of one and put it back in the other.

'David, do you remember? There's this glorious bit in the book . . .'

Oh fuck this job! And what's more Stephen Daldry's directing. Which means we're all going to be here for the next few years. I can't even count the number of times I've come to Berlin. I took this script because they promised me it was going to get made. Quickly. I'd read the book eight years previously, as soon as it came out, and I wanted to do it, partly because it was a great book, and partly because the moment I read it, I knew how to do it. In my experience, if you don't know at once you never know. Only eight years on, I can't remember why on earth I thought it was going to be simple. What was I thinking? 'It's very simple. I'm going to write this film about a boy who unknowingly has an affair with an older war criminal.' Oh yeah? Simple or what?

People say film is a mosaic. They may be right. But to me it's a duvet. An old eiderdown. Always with a lump. All you do by rewriting is move the lump around. As soon as you deal with it in one part of the film, it pops up in another. You spend months, or if you're working with Stephen Daldry, *years* moving the lump to another part of the film.

That's how it feels, or rather how it has been feeling as I eat my meticulous breakfast at the Concorde Hotel. The

Concorde is full of managers from companies like Siemens and Lufthansa, gliding towards power-point presentations after stashing away glittering stacks of cheese and ham, of *Wurst und Eierspeise*. The prices are much lower than in any other capital city in Western Europe, the food more generous. Here there is bounty, there is an executive banquet of life-giving juices, and all for the price of a stiff magazine. The city's meant to be bankrupt. In fact, that's one of the two things everyone knows about Berlin. The Mayor is gay and the city is bankrupt. 'Berlin is poor but sexy,' the Mayor keeps saying. But 'poor' doesn't really say it, not when the city owes fifty-four billion euros and unemployment's at seventeen per cent. Some of its attempts to offset its debt by disposing of its assets have not been successful. Joseph Goebbels's country house did not sell.

Of course by now I've worked out exactly why I couldn't find the Schiller Theater. Believe it or not, what was once the best-known theatre in West Berlin has been closed down. In 1993, its five hundred and fifty employees were let go. It was still selling over two hundred thousand tickets a season. But when Berlin was unified, everyone agreed there were too many orchestras, too many opera houses, too many galleries – in short too much art. The city was, in that chilling McKinseyite phrase, 'super-served'. So the weakest went to the wall, in a kind of vengeful art-cull of which our own Arts Council can only dream.

This morning, as we drive past the golden walls of the one arts institution in Berlin which nobody dares touch, I remember a moment from that film festival in the nineties, when someone finally said to me, 'You do know that as a member of the jury you're entitled to a free ticket at the Berlin Philharmonic?' Thereafter, I went every night, as much for the visual pleasure – the famous string section rippling like corn in the breeze – as for the sound. I saw Alfred Brendel, the model of a great artist, play a Beethoven piano concerto in the first half of the programme, then modestly take a seat just in front of us for the second, because he wanted to hear Abbado conduct Brahms as much as we did. Our row applauded him. He looked embarrassed.

Today I'm late on location, not that anyone notices, except for Ivana, the chief make-up artist. '*Guten Morgen, David. Hast du dein Frühstück gegessen?*' Ivana is as Anglophone as I am, but we're both ashamed to be working in a country where you don't speak a word. We're trying to do something about it. '*Ja, Ivana, ich habe Eier und Speck gegessen.*' '*Mit Kaffee?*' '*Ja.*' '*Viefiel Kaffee?*' '*Drei Tasse Kaffee.*' We go through this ritual every morning. The crew look at us pityingly, but we tell ourselves that they appreciate the gesture. As well as looking after our actors, Ivana also 'does' Gordon Brown. It's Ivana who brushed him up for the leadership of his party. Back at home, there is speculation that as Prime Minister Brown will now call an early general election. But Ivana is confident that it's out of the question while she's tied up working in Germany. 'He's not going to call an election with that haircut.'

As it happens, we are filming at the Hohenschönhausen prison on Genslerstrasse. This has been a hugely difficult location to secure. The prison is in the suburb of Lichtenberg. Although Lichtenberg was a busy mixed housing and industrial area in East Berlin, for almost forty years large parts of it were represented by a blank space on city maps. It did not officially exist. Today, as well as being a museum, Hohenschönhausen is also a graveyard. Immediately after the war, it served as a Soviet detention camp where four thousand German citizens were held without charge. Three thousand are buried on the site. In the 1960s, the prison was the Stasi's centre for psychological torture.

The day of Operation Rose was August 13th 1961.
Without warning, four hundred trucks headed from the
East German countryside at midnight to throw up a ring
of barbed wire, formally to divide the city. The border
was sealed while the world was on holiday. The Mayor
of West Berlin, Willie Brandt, was in Nuremberg. The
President of America, John Kennedy, was sunning himself
on Cape Cod. And the Prime Minister of Britain, Harold
Macmillan, was on the Yorkshire moors, celebrating the
first day of the grouse-shooting season. At the news of
the construction, Macmillan continued to shoot. The *fait
accompli* was achieved with dazzling speed. Protesters
gathered at the Brandenburg Gate, making gaps in the
wire, and pulling a few people bodily through. But with
no Western leader daring to call for insurrection in the
East, Berlin was divided. In the following months, seven
thousand people would be rounded up and brought to
Hohenschönhausen for a programme of sensory
deprivation, isolation and secret trial.

It's unsettling, you feel shallow, everyone can feel it –
how can you not? – making your fiction, telling your
little story in what was once the heart of the apparatus
of oppression. 'We shouldn't be filming here,' says the
cinematographer. Today the prison is, as usual, open to
tour groups, open to students. It's a condition of our
filming that we work around them, so we wander, carrying
our cappuccinos, stepping over cables and scaffolding for
the big lights, while schoolchildren laze on the steps. A
couple of girls are laughing as they compare the shortness
of the little pieces of frayed denim which serve as their
skirts, and speculate on how much further they can go,
and still have anything round their middles at all.

Without my noticing, the day has passed. Sometimes
a screenwriter's barely needed on set – a little dialogue
streamlined here and there – but Stephen is my friend,

and I like to whisper in his ear. As the afternoon goes by, the air gets warmer and Stephen becomes more absorbed. For once, I can't feel the pull of his anxiety. So I have no particular intention as I walk out of the prison yard. Most of the tour buses have gone. Which way is Berlin?

For no reason I decide to go right, the traffic streaming home in both directions. As an adolescent I used to enjoy this, going to a strange city and scaring myself by getting lost. Tonight there's a circus on one side, a row of Turkish shops on the other, the men gathered at plastic tables to play cards and drink beer. There's a rhythm to walking, so that walking itself becomes the point. Maybe an hour goes by, maybe two. I seem to have confused Potsdamer Platz with Alexanderplatz and gone the wrong way. But what is the wrong way when you're not going anywhere? Then suddenly the most extraordinary coincidence. I look up and I see the word 'Bandol'. *Bandol!*

How do I explain this? There's backstory here, as Americans say. Every summer we go on holiday to a house in France which happens, yes, to be right next to a seaside town called Bandol. My wife is French and her oldest friend is Martine Gouty, whose daughter is called Elsa. Elsa's about thirty and she gave up a good job in Paris in order to go and live in Berlin. She's going out with an German architect called Fred. I'll tell you, like so many others, Elsa liked the idea of living in Berlin. She makes enough money to live by working three nights a week deciding who can and can't be admitted to a club. That's her job. Her mother can't see much future in it, but it's what Elsa wants to do. 'For now,' she says. 'Just for now.'

Anyway, last year in Bandol when Fred and Elsa came to dinner, I asked Fred what he'd built, and he said 'A restaurant in Berlin called Bandol.' In fact, he said, he and Elsa hang out there all the time. So do their friends.

And so, goodness me, here it is, looking like . . . well, how do I describe it? You'd certainly know an architect had done it, because it's futuristic. It's very severe, industrial materials only, concrete and metal beams, no concessions to anything pansy like decoration, and oddest of all – I've opened the door and gone in – it's the size of a cupboard under the stairs. How can a restaurant make money with fifteen seats?

I look at my watch, it's eight o'clock, and every table is full. But they'll let me sit on a stool at the service counter. I'm directly opposite the cook, who like everyone in this place is young. I don't mean young, I mean young compared to me. Probably most people here are in their thirties, with full heads of hair and warm smiles. Some of the boys look in love with the boys, some of the girls with the girls, some of the boys with the girls, in fact everyone is with who they want to be, and the food's going down well. They all look as if they're talking about – well, art, I suppose. And clubs. The sound of their talk is lively but there's none of the screaming and forced laughter you get in London restaurants, so it's easy for me to get out my paperback, which is a Michael Connolly, and settle down to read.

Time goes by, dishes arrive, clients come and go, then at some point I look up and realise I'm incredibly happy. No, more than that. For the first time ever I feel I've got a grip on Berlin. Put it another way, I've got a theory. I believe I know what Berlin is about.

It's about hanging out with your friends.

By chance, I'm the only person in the restaurant without any friends, but I'm still finally plugging into Berlin. How can I have missed anything so obvious? My paperback is excellent, the food is excellent, I've had some delicious scallops, followed by a rich murky bouillabaisse, full of sea grit and bits and pieces, and basically I don't see how life could be any better.

All right. I'm out on the street. It's eleven o'clock. I don't actually know where I am. The sign says 'Torstrasse'. Some taxis go by, but I prefer to resume walking. I think I forgot to mention that the food at Bandol had seemed particularly familiar, particularly comforting because it was served with the wines of the Bandol region, which, for those of you who care about these things, have a growing reputation. The outstanding wine of Bandol, without any question, is the Château Pibarnon. Just to be clear: I'm not walking along a Berlin street having an epiphany *because* I've drunk a bottle of red wine. No, I've drunk a bottle of red wine *and* I'm having an epiphany.

I don't know if you know the effect of exercise when taken with Château Pibarnon, but to a layman at least it begins to feel as if extra oxygen is in your blood. You feel aerated – that's the word – and, as I walk, I'm beginning to notice a curious thing. Berlin is full of Bandols. I don't mean literally, I don't mean there are other branches of the excellent restaurant Bandol. What I mean is that I am passing dozens of very small restaurants full of very happy people. It's as if Bandol has been a sort of template and every night the template is replicated all over the city.

Now I get it, now I understand.

You find like-minded people, you find your group and you stick with them, so you won't be challenged. 'For now,' you say. 'Just for now.'

You may well ask what kind of pathetic person it is who needs a theory to be happy. But there it is. Now I have my theory, I feel much better. I'm thinking I should have got out of my car months ago. And then as if one coincidence were not enough for an evening, here's a second. I turn the corner and – blow me! – there's the Theater am Schiffbauerdamm. I have goose-bumps. It's rare you can say 'I'm thrilled' and mean it. It's a large building, in brown stone, with an imposing forecourt. It's right by the river and on the top is a revolving neon sign. I can't believe it. It's midnight and this is my first sight of the Berliner Ensemble.

Again, you may say that it's a weird sort of accomplishment to have worked forty years as a political playwright and never to have seen the Berliner Ensemble. I'm a Catholic who's never been to Rome. They made their groundbreaking visit to the Palace Theatre in London in August 1956. I was nine. Theatre workers of my generation grew up in awe of Brecht, because he was presented to us as a writer who had entirely reconceived the theatre of ideas, stripping it of piss and wind. Later he was looked on less favourably, as someone who had made an accommodation with tyranny in order to be allowed to have his own theatre. Just after he won the Stalin Peace Prize, Brecht died, in his words, '*etwas reduziert*' – somewhat reduced. By coincidence, he was making plans for a production of *Waiting for Godot*, and had already put thick black lines through what he regarded as the the over-writing. Because the cemetery he nominated was full, already-buried bodies were dug up and moved to accommodate him.

Looking at this formidable institution, with its air of glacial confidence, its innumerable posters for classic plays, it's hard not to be shocked by the sight of a temple of *Kultur* set among the garish shopping malls of the new Berlin. I had always pictured the Ensemble down a gloomy, darkened side street, next to some appropriately atmospheric lamp posts. But no, here it stands, lit by the reflections of the Coca-Cola signs, the ads for Lancôme and Prada and Gucci, a redoubt of worthiness in a blaze of consumerism.

And now I actually look at it, what am I reminded of? Why, there's only one theatre as big as this, as solid as this: it's the Comédie Française, the house of Moliere. Same thing, surely? Molière, the satirist of the bourgeoisie, the moral provocateur, smoothed out into a national treasure. It used to annoy Caryl Churchill when people claimed that her satire on eighties greed *Serious Money* drew an audience largely composed of city bankers, who roared appreciatively at her fierce condemnation of their trade. Caryl's basic point: *it wasn't true*. The audience was actually quite mixed. Yes, a few bankers came, but not that many. And they did enjoy it, but not that much. But the right-wing press relished talking up their occasional presence, because, of course, the right-wing press adores the idea that all art is emasculated by the society it's created in.

But – to be fair – standing, looking at the theatre, seeing the name of Bertolt Brecht, the one-time rebel and revolutionary on the repertory slate next to Shakespeare and Schiller and Goethe and Chekhov and Ibsen and Strindberg and Lessing – it's hard not to admit, things do seem a very long way away from radicalism and outrage and the sensational first night of *The Threepenny Opera*, which took place exactly where I'm standing.

Now I'm walking, walking on, thinking, what's next? I'm coming to the Brandenburg Gate, which is brilliantly lit. Six people there. That's the joy of it. You have the city to yourself. One of the most famous sites in the world, and it's empty.

I can go on, I can walk all night if I choose, along the long straight road, the Ost-West Achse, which cuts through Tiergarten, the enormous park at the centre of

the city. The Nazis used this avenue as a landing strip
when all their airports had been bombed. But I admit I'm
weakening. There's lush foliage on both sides – suddenly
it seems more like a forest than a park – and it's a long
time since I passed another human being. I'm getting
jumpy. I'm expecting Peter Lorre to appear at any
moment and kill me for drugs. But also, I suppose if I'm
honest, I'm torn between satisfaction in having a view of
Berlin, and disappointment in what that view is.

My best-ever visit to Berlin was just after the Wall came
down. We came with our friend Ilana, who's from
Cologne. She'd never been. On that heady weekend,
visiting bookshops, galleries and bars, it seemed as if the
city were filling up with every poet, anarchist, punk,
pornographer and hippy from all over Europe. It looked
poised to take off in new and wilder directions. A city
with so much history was shifting once more to let
history take another fascinating turn. But today, that's
not how it feels. No, today it's as if the city's taking a
holiday from history. 'We had enough history. See where
it got us.' Berlin, once the city of polarity, of East and
West, of democracy and communism, of fascism and
resistance, the twentieth-century battleground of art and
politics is now the city of the provisional. And that's
exactly why people like it.

It's not about ideas. It's about lifestyle.

I wake up the next morning and decide it's time to go
home. What am I doing here? Not very much. Future
generations are going to judge us, and they're going to
judge us harshly. Between 1989 and 2001 the West
missed its greatest opportunity. At the start, our Prime
Minister, Margaret Thatcher, was on the wrong side on
two of the greatest issues of her day. She did nothing to
help the ANC end apartheid; and she fought German
reunification. She was morally derelict and deserves to

be condemned for it. She didn't move fast enough. But then nobody did. Between the ending of one Cold War, and the beginning of another, between the defeat of communism and its replacement by militant Islam as the West's readily convenient enemy, there was a real chance. International relations, the creative remaking of relations between countries irrespective of wealth or ideology, was briefly possible. Briefly. Nothing got done. What new world order?

My day on the set speeds by. The work's lighter today, and everyone's in good spirits. It's Friday, and the last British Airways flight back to London goes at 7.45. I like this flight, because I always run into someone I know. You check in at Tegel, then when you go through to the bar, it's always full of British actors, scoffing crisps and those little biscuits the shape of fish. Years ago, these people would have been charming audiences in regional reps, offering their Falstaffs and Lady Bracknells. But things have changed. Nowadays British actors are dispatched from Heathrow all over the world, to offer the struts of good character acting to hold up the roof for dimpled American movie stars. Berlin is a big centre for international film-making – something to do with tax breaks – so I can guarantee on any Friday night to run into a couple of acquaintances at the end of their week's commute, looking forward to a weekend at home with their partners. Sure enough, tonight, look, there's old ———, he was recently in a play of mine and we haven't yet had the enjoyable conversation when we badmouth the director. And isn't that ———? We wanted her in a play, but the dates didn't work out.

And so it is we settle in, a group of us actually, not really minding that the plane is late. 'How's yours going?' 'So how's yours?' Nearly everyone tonight is on the Tom Cruise movie, which is about von Stauffenberg who led the revolt against the Führer in 1944. Cruise plays von Stauffenberg, and British character actors play all the rest. David Bamber is playing Hitler. At one point I casually ask one of the actors which film he's in. 'I'm making a film about the historical plot to kill David Bamber.'

The point's too obvious, it scarcely needs making, but I'll make it all the same. These are people I've known and loved all my life. For me, the transit lounge at Tegel is my Bandol.

But even here, it isn't simple. You can never quite relax in Berlin. Just after they call the plane and we decide to grab another packet of biscuits, one of the actors asks me how long I've been coming here. 'Oh, a long time actually, maybe for eighteen months.' He looks at me a moment, then asks the inevitable question. 'So have you heard of this place called the Kit-Kat Club?' I smile. 'As a matter of fact I have.' 'And have you been?' 'Do you know, I haven't. I've heard a lot about it. But I'm a happily married man, why on earth would I go to the Kit-Kat Club?'

I know this actor really well. In fact I've known him for years. And he knows me, so he also knows that I mean what I say. But then, remembering I'm supposed to be a dramatist, I add, 'Of course I'd go to the Kit-Kat Club if I could just watch.' And now the actor's look really darkens, his eye is cold, and there's a sort of steel, an admonishment, as if he knew me better than I know myself. 'No, David. You can't just watch. You have to take part.'

I'm lying in bed next morning. And I'm thinking, 'Lucky Stephen Daldry. He's directing the film, and I'm not.' Is that what I've wanted all along? To direct the film? But worse, Stephen's in Berlin and I'm not. I'm briefly jealous. Maybe they're right. Maybe everyone's right. I should buy an apartment in Kreuzburg. It's the coming area, and property's ridiculously cheap. That's it. I'll buy an apartment in Kreuzburg.

But hold on a minute.

When would I go? And where would I be on my way to when I went?

WALL

All right. Let's be serious, let's think about this.

Please: please, consider the state of affairs, consider the desperation, consider the depth of the despair. A country has reached a point at which eighty-four per cent of its people are in favour of building a wall along its borders.

Have you ever known anything of which eighty-four per cent of people were in favour? And yet there it is, over four-fifths of a nation – can you imagine that figure? – saying something completely bizarre. The Berlin Wall was built to keep people in. This one, they say, is being built to keep people out.

You might call this an extraordinary state of affairs. Hardly a normal state of affairs. And that's the word you hear all the time in the Middle East. 'Normal'. The Palestinians ask, 'When will we have a normal life?' And so do the Israelis. Indeed, the Israeli state was founded in 1948 with the principal ambition of being normal, of being a normal place like any other. The Palestinians call the foundation of the Israeli state the *nakbeh*: the disaster. And now sixty years later Israel believes itself, in the frequently expressed view of the majority, in need of a wall.

Except, of course, they don't call it a wall. They call it a fence.

It's one of those things, there seem to be so many, don't there? – I'm thinking of abortion, or armed revolt – where the words you use – pro-life/pro-choice, terrorist/ freedom fighter – tell the world which way you think.

Words become flags, they announce which side you're on. In this case, literally. The Israelis call it the *gader ha' harfrada*, which in Hebrew means 'separation fence'. The Palestinians don't call it that. Not at all. They call it *jidar al-fasl al 'unsun* which in Arabic means 'racial segregation wall'.

OK, let's go coolly into this, shall we? If I use one phrase or another, forgive me, it does not imply I am partisan. I have acquaintances on both sides of the fence and on both sides of the wall. 'I hate the wall,' say my Israeli friends. 'I regret it.' 'I'm ashamed of the wall.' 'I drive for miles so that I don't have to see it. But it works. Eighty per cent of terrorist attacks against Israel have stopped. Have been stopped. Am I not meant to be pleased about that?'

Very well. I shall seek to describe the history of the wall.

On June 1st 2001, nine months into the second *intifada*, a suicide bomber, Saeed Hotari, crossed into Israel from the West Bank and, studded with nails and ball bearings, exploded himself at the entrance to the Dolphinarium discotheque on the beach in Tel Aviv, killing twenty-one civilians, most of them high school students. A further hundred and thirty-two people were injured. In response to the massacre, a grass-roots movement grew up all over Israel calling itself 'Fence for Life'. They argued, as the Prime Minister Yitzak Rabin had argued ten years earlier, that the only way of protecting the country from infiltration by terrorists was by sealing itself off, by removing the points of friction between the two communities. But separation would not be a purely military tactic. No, before he was murdered by a fellow Israeli, Rabin had been arguing something much more radical, something existential. 'We have to decide on separation as a philosophy.'

30

There it is. Not just a wall. A wall would be a fact. But this wall is a philosophy, what one observer has called 'a political code for shutting up shop'.

Construction began in 2002. The original plan was that the fence should stretch a full four hundred and eighty-six miles, the entire length of Israel's eastern border. The current estimate for its final completion is some time around the end of 2010. Varying in width between thirty and one hundred and fifty metres, this two-billion-dollar combination of trenches, electronic fences, ditches, watchtowers, concrete slabs, checkpoints, patrol roads and razor coil is priced at around two million dollars per kilometre. It will one day be over four times as long as the Berlin Wall and in some places twice as high. Seventy-five acres of greenhouses and twenty-three miles of irrigation pipes have already been destroyed on the Palestinian side. Three thousand, seven hundred and five acres of Palestinian land have been confiscated, some of it so that the wall may run yards away from Palestinian hamlets and villages. Already, a hundred and two thousand trees have been cut down to clear its path.

It is, says an Israeli friend, an acknowledgement of failure. 'History has not followed the course we might have wished.' Another way of putting it, later the same evening, after a few drinks in one of the big beachside hotels which are beginning to make the Bauhaus quarter of Tel Aviv look like Florida: 'You do have to ask yourself: I'm not sure Ben-Gurion would be thrilled.'

From the start the exact route has been controversial. The most obvious path for it to have followed would have been along the international border, established in 1949 between Israel and Jordan, and known to all parties as the Green Line. But, in fact, eighty-five per cent of its intended route is inside the West Bank. The fence snakes and coils, departing eastward from the Green Line in places by just two hundred metres, but in other places by as much as twenty-two kilometres where it goes inland to collect up and protect Israeli settlements established far inside the occupied territory. Sometimes it takes in fertile Palestinian agricultural land and water wells, leaving Palestinian farmers without access to their own fields. Some 140,200 Israeli settlers will be living between the fence and the Green Line. Ninety-three thousand Palestinians will be caught on the wrong side of the wall.

For that reason the fence is seen by its opponents not as what it claims to be – a security measure – but more as a land-grab, the delineation of a de facto claim, an attempt, like the steady expansion of the Israeli-controlled parts of Jerusalem, to do what is known as 'change the facts on the ground'. At the outset of the campaign, supporters of Fence for Life insisted that the wall should be a barrier, not a border. It was not to be used as a bargaining tactic in any future negotiation for a final status agreement. But even Israelis have found this intention hard to credit. The outgoing Israeli Prime Minister Ehud Olmert has admitted that had he survived in the job he would have sought to set Israeli permanent borders by 2010 – and that the border 'would run along or close to the barrier'.

Even the most ardent supporters of the fence admit that it is, like the siege of Gaza, a source of huge inconvenience. But they argue, in the words of one defender, that 'the deaths of Israelis caused by terror are permanent and irreversible, whereas the hardships faced by the Palestinians are temporary and reversible'. The International Court of Justice in the Hague had a different view. On July 9th 2004 it ruled by fourteen votes to one that 'The construction of a wall being built by Israel, the occupying power, in the occupied Palestinian territory . . . [is] contrary to international law. Israel is under an obligation to cease forthwith the works of construction . . . to dismantle the works forthwith . . . to make reparation for all the damage caused by the construction of the wall . . .' Professor Sari Nusseibeh of Al-Quds University, puts it most pithily: 'You put someone in a cage, then when he starts screaming, as any normal person would, you use his violent temper as justification for putting him in the cage in the first place. The wall is a perfect crime. It creates the violence it was ostensibly built to prevent.'

*

Tell you what, to give you an idea what it's like, one morning I'm setting out from Ramallah. Ramallah houses the Palestinian Authority, which controls the West Bank – as opposed to Hamas which was elected in Gaza in January 2006. Ramallah is a government town, and like all government towns – like DC, like Canberra – a bit bland, a bit boring. Today I'm setting out with a couple of friends; one is from London, the other to whom the car belongs, and to whom also therefore the crucial number plate, is Palestinian. The evening before, in Jerusalem, I've been taking tea with an Israeli intellectual who outlines what he regards as the defining paradox of Israel: to the world it seems powerful and aggressive, yet to itself it seems weak and frail.

Israel, he says, has no real confidence in its own survival. 'Israelis have a very fragile sense of the future,' he says. 'It's incredible but the country itself still feels provisional. Of what other state can this be said? I notice when I am in Britain that you plan for 2038, you say there will be this railway or that airport. But no Israeli plans so far ahead without feeling a pang in his heart which asks whether we shall be here at all. We look so strong from the outside, we have such a large army, so many nuclear weapons, we're so certain in our expansion, and yet from the inside it doesn't feel like that. We feel our being is not guaranteed. You might say we have imported from the Diaspora the Jewish disease – a sense of rootlessness, an ability to adapt and make do, but not to settle. After sixty years, Israel is not yet a home.'

I'm thinking of his words next day – secure but insecure, strong but uncertain – as the three of us come to a road block. It's a dusty spot, featureless, in the middle of nowhere – or would be featureless if it weren't for the run of high concrete slabs on our left-hand side. The wall. We join a long line of cars which we are told has been here for fifteen minutes. The drivers have turned their engines off, and they sit on the roofs or the bonnets, smoking cigarettes and talking. Yes, this is what happens every day. A daily event. For those who are allowed to go back and forth more than once daily, a more-than-once daily event. The soldiers are letting only one side go through at a time. So we sit for a further twenty minutes, cars coming at us from the opposite direction, and then very slowly, insolently, the Israelis, carrying machine guns, move to our side of the road, and for no reason, begin to let us move.

I say 'for no reason' but probably there is a reason. And nobody imagines it has anything to do with security. After all, the road stretches empty in either direction, and the checkpoint is not short-staffed. Why, then, are Israeli soldiers wasting time by holding back one line of traffic which they could perfectly well let through, while they permit the flow of another? Why are they doing this? The answer seems clear. They are doing it because they can. 'If we choose to delay you, we shall. We have the right to delay you. We have the right to render your life meaningless.'

Inevitably, as we drive on, delayed, I'm still thinking back to the famous writer in the suburb of Jerusalem, the gorgeous evening light, the tea, the home-baked sweet biscuits, the profound leafy calm of his home. 'We look strong but we feel weak.' Is that the reason, then, for the harassment, for the needless harassment, for the pointless insistence that daily life is as frustrating as possible? For what the Palestinians call their collective punishment? How, you wonder, are the Palestinians to *know* that the Israelis feel weak, when all they can see is the Israelis acting strong? When Tony Blair was appointed Middle East envoy in June 2007 there were five hundred and twenty-one Israeli checkpoints on the West Bank. Today there are six hundred and ninety-nine.

Another thing my Israeli friend said: 'The occupation degrades them. But it also degrades us.'

'We need a wall because we want a normal life,' says one lot. 'Our life will never be normal for as long as there's a wall,' says the other. A great deal has changed since I started coming here over ten years ago. Both sides now agree that a solution is inevitable. There will be an end to all this. 'The old arguments,' says one Israeli friend, 'between Left and Right are over. The Left won.' Everywhere, there is an acceptance that things must move on. 'We cannot go on as we are. There must be a solution.' You hear it on both sides. Trouble is, this being the Middle East, and especially after the latest war, neither side agrees on what that solution is. Just as Israelis finally shrug and concede that, 'After all, a two-state solution is indeed inevitable, yes, the two countries must one day exist side by side,' so at that very moment, the Palestinians, or at the least the ones I meet, adopt the same weary largesse: 'All right, at last we are saying it: we are ready to share one state with the Israelis.'

That's how it is, or that's how it seems to me. Israeli prime ministers come in as hawks, promising security crackdowns and military build-ups. They leave office convinced that the occupation is unsustainable, that the cost of occupying another people for ever cannot be borne. 'A new generation of Israelis,' I am told everywhere, 'has grown up. They're more cosmopolitan. They travel the world. Yes, they're committed to Israel, emotionally they're committed to its survival, but on the other hand they want a good reason for living here rather in California. If we can't give them one, they'll go elsewhere.' The socialist idealism in which Israel was founded is long gone. In its place, a hard-headed practicality. But if it's hard-headed practicality you want, if it's beaches and machine guns, you can find those anywhere in the world. What will make the young choose to live in Israel?

Sure, the religious-minded know the answer to that question – even the putting of the question offends them – but do the secular? It's the same on the other side, fear of a rising fundamentalism forcing open-minded Palestinians towards an accommodation they were once less ready to make. In conversation, Palestinians don't quite have the easy generosity the Israelis have – after all, the occupied never do, do they? It's a different tone. But even so. The rise of Hamas scares the shit out of everyone. Hamas are popular as much in reaction to the corruption of the PLO as for any positive enthusiasm for their methods. So – just as good British socialists never spoke ill of the Soviet Union in front of strangers – so also many Palestinians don't talk much about Hamas. It's disloyal. But few people on the West Bank are exactly defending them either.

One evening not long ago we'd been at a party in Ramallah. It was a sophisticated kind of affair. A whole sheep was served. A man who used to run the Body Shop in Riyadh had rolled up his sleeves. 'Give me the sheep,' he said. 'I'll do it.' Turns out he does it at least once a month, tearing apart a fragrant stuffed sheep with his fingers, and serving it up for guests. The meat is fatty, warm, delicious. Dismembering is a skill and I love watching. At the end only the bare skeleton is left. The only drawback being, as I load a second plate, that another guest is meanwhile telling me about a Hamas torture technique against citizens of Gaza suspected of informing. As follows.

The victim is shown a wall on which a staircase is drawn, and at the top is a drawing of a bicycle. The victim is told to go and get the bicycle. He says he can't get the bicycle because it's a drawing. He is then told if he doesn't bring the bicycle downstairs he will be beaten. 'I can't get it. It's a drawing.'

Or. A variation. In Palestine there are two television channels, one run by Hamas, the other by the Authority. A remote control is drawn on the wall. The prisoner is told to change the television from the lying PLO channel which is currently playing to the heroic Hamas channel. The prisoner replies he cannot change the channel because the remote control is a drawing. He is told, 'Change the channel or you'll be beaten.'

All right, OK, what does that prove? I'm asking myself, as we drive on. Hamas aren't very nice. You wouldn't be nice if you lived under permanent siege. But the ingenuity chills me. It's so thought out, so intellectual even, to ask someone to go get a drawing. Is this what we're dealing with? So much thought put into a simple means of torture? Or am I missing the point? Is this some metaphor for how Palestinians feel? That everything is a drawing? Everything is unattainable? You reach. You can't get it.

I need to know the answer because right now we're heading for Nablus. I don't know why, but my whole life I've wanted to go to Nablus. I like the sound of it. Sometimes it feels that I've wanted to go ever since Emperor Vespasian founded it in 72 AD. Only he named it Neapolis: a classic Byzantine, then Ottoman city nestling beside sheer-cliffed hills. But we can't go along the tarmac road because the Israelis control access. Soldiers have already turned us away a couple of times, so each time we set off in new directions, winding back, climbing, always in search of the one illicit route, unguarded, which takes you into the back of the city.

And all the time, at the top of every hill, it seems, there's yet another Israeli settlement.

Again, from yesterday, I recall the exasperation of the writer: 'There are only a quarter of a million settlers,' he said. 'They're nothing. They're the size of one average Israeli town. And seventy-five per cent of them aren't there out of any religious conviction. They're there because they're paid to be. The housing is cheap and the schooling is good. Pay them some more and they'll leave. And yet,' he says bitterly, 'for forty years the national debate has been centred round the fate of these few people. It's time we moved on.'

He draws my attention to an article in the *New York Times* which interviews those non-religious Israeli settlers who find themselves caught on the wrong side of the wall, and now owning property which is effectively valueless. It is estimated that forty thousand wish to leave, to move back to pre-'67 Israel. Monika Yzchaki has lived in Mevo Dotan for fifteen years. 'I can name forty families who want to leave but are afraid to say it out loud. Nobody understands there are a lot of us who are not extremists or crazy. Now I have to show a passport at the barrier to get home.' In the settlement of Karmei Shomron, Benny Raz leads the movement for compensation. He has lived there for fifteen years, and his religious neighbours are furious with him for wanting to leave. 'I get threatening phone calls telling me I am going to be killed. Today,' he says, 'I carry a gun because I am afraid of the Jews, not of the Arabs.'

My friend has spoken of the settlers with a wave of the hand as if, 'Oh forget about the settlers, they'll be dealt with.' But, in fact, it isn't till you travel on the West Bank, it isn't till you look, it isn't till you see where the settlers are – literally all around you – that you think, 'I'm not sure this is quite as simple as people say.' Because, you see, sometimes you look up to that hilltop, and then the next one, and then the one beyond that, and there aren't even houses, just caravans, the caravans arriving to plant a new community, and then no sooner are the foundations down than they move on to plant another. They're called settlements, but in fact they're plantations. And – hey, another question – if this *is* the Holy Land, if the land is indeed holy, why are they making it so ugly? Why are they destroying the savage wildness of the hills with ticky-tack houses and radar masts?

And that's what I feel in Jerusalem as well. Jerusalem used to be the spiritual capital – after all, that's what the argument was about. You could feel it, on every street corner, you could feel the history, but now with the hideous wall and the overbuilding and desecration of the landscape – I mean, what is going on? Aren't they destroying the very quality for which the city was meant to be precious? Aren't they killing the thing they love? Or is that my problem? Am I just a decadent Westerner who can't help thinking spirituality must have something to do with beauty? Am I the only idiot who still confuses religion with aesthetics? Oh I see, was the whole Renaissance just a European detour, a historical mistake, an irrelevance? Jerusalem used to be beautiful. Now it isn't. It used to take your breath away. Now it doesn't. But does that matter? What's my complaint exactly? That things are insufficiently medieval? As far as I'm concerned, Jerusalem is spoilt – how can it not be spoilt? It has a bloody great concrete wall – but then Jerusalem was never intended for me. It was intended for believers.

So – look again, look to the hills, and you can see why the Palestinians consider the settlements not a religious phenomenon but a network of control. Because that's what they look like. Watching over us. And another thing, by the way: we're lost. There's a certain amount of Palestinian macho going on, on my right, my friend boasting, 'I know the way.' Actually, he doesn't. So a tall man, pencil-thin, with a moustache and a cigarette, a kind of oriental George Orwell, has got out of his Volkswagen. 'You want to get into Nablus?' he says, roaring with laughter at our uselessness, as if he encounters this problem five times a day. 'I'll get you into Nablus. Follow me.' And off he goes, cheery, farting petrol fumes: the camaraderie of the road, the camaraderie of occupation, the impossibility of daily life turned into survivors' humour. Orwell driving like a maniac, us hard pressed to follow. Across a few unmarked tracks, then we turn a corner, and shit! It's Nablus. So that's where they've been hiding it. A forty-minute journey has taken over three hours, but it's still Nablus.

I don't entirely understand this. People always ask: how do you choose the subjects you write about? I have a glib answer. Why did Bacon paint popes? Meaning: the artist doesn't choose the subject, the subject chooses the artist. 'Go to Rwanda,' said my American agent, when ten years ago I first proposed a play about Israel/Palestine. 'Better still, go to Kashmir. Now there's a dispute nobody understands. Throw some light on Kashmir.' But unfortunately it doesn't work like that. Recently, I found myself writing about Berlin because I don't understand it. Now I want to write about Israel/Palestine because I do. No, hold on, let me rephrase, that's a preposterous claim, nobody *understands* the Middle East – but put it this way: I recognise it. It answers to something in me.

And that's what I feel, this is the summit of the feeling, looking down at Vespasian's town for the first time, the town of Joseph's tomb and of Jacob's well. Nablus, a city with a hundred and eighty thousand residents, surrounded by six Israeli checkpoints, fourteen Jewish settlements and twenty-six settlement outposts which are illegal even under Israeli law. Nablus, the city that everyone says will be the crucial testing ground for the future of the Palestinian Authority on the West Bank: once a home to the Fatah-based Al-Aqsa Martyrs Brigade, but now with a Mayor, Adly Yaish, a graduate of Liverpool University, who, though not a member of Hamas, nevertheless ran on their ticket and got seventy-three per cent of the vote in 2005. Since then he has spent fifteen months of his term as Mayor in Israeli jails, without ever being charged with anything. Nine times Israeli judges have ordered his release.

'Nablus,' Yaish says, 'used to be the commercial capital of the Palestinians, now it's the capital of poverty. It used to be the biggest city on the West Bank, now it's the biggest village.' Nablus, a trading centre which is no longer allowed to trade because – problem for a trading centre – nobody's allowed to go there. Here we are, by devious means, passing through grey stone arches into the countless alleys of the old covered market. This could be Marrakech: row upon row of raw meat, and fresh fruit, and flies and umbrellas and clothes and perfumes and spices, and dogs wandering, and children, and bubbling pans of *kanafeh*, of which the locals are famously proud: layers of Nabulsi cheese boiled with sugar, dyed dayglo-orange and scattered with crushed pistachios. Too rich for my blood. Even the smell sticks my tongue to the roof of my mouth. Up to eighty per cent of the citizens of this town are unemployed. So there are few customers, and the prices are half they are in Jerusalem. In the corner, a Biblical *hammam*, up a short alley, nothing but steam and stones.

Oh yes, I'm happy here, this is the kind of place which makes me happy. You can lose yourself. Now we've come upon what seems to be the most famous café, at the centre of the market, looking like one of the greenhouses at Kew. Before renovation, of course. Flat-planed walls of cracked glass and rotting timber, giving out onto a sunny courtyard. The Sheikh Qasim Café used to be the fashionable place, the hub, where everyone went, the Ivy of Nablus. Now, with just five of its four hundred wooden chairs occupied, it looks like a film set, a stage play, maybe at the Glasgow Cits, one of those expressionist jobbies – peeling paint, the wild romanticism of abandonment and decay. Unless something happens soon, unless the Israelis relax their grip, unless peace comes to the Middle East, the soil will reclaim this place. And quickly. We order Turkish coffee. Then I turn.

On the wall, in this decaying spot, the only new thing: a bright gleaming poster of Saddam Hussein.

It's one of those moments. I know as soon as I look, I'm never going to forget. 'I'll never forget that day in Nablus when I saw that poster of Saddam Hussein.' How do you react to that? If you were going to choose a hero, could you choose a worse? If you were going to choose a future, could you so completely misconceive it? If you were going to choose a leader to take you precisely nowhere, could you do better than Saddam Hussein? Just for starters, Hussein stood for everything Hamas doesn't. Secularisation. A non-religious state. Have they thought about that? Let alone his matchless record for killing Arabs. My mind flashes back to Cherie Blair who once fell into one of those stupid media rows for saying that if you deny the young hope, no wonder they blow themselves up. You can understand it, she said, when you come to Palestine. Maybe, but could she understand this? You choose as your poster boy someone who has done the world, and the Arab world above all, nothing but harm. The master of mass graves and untold massacres.

I turn to my companion. 'What is this?' I ask. 'My enemy's enemy is my friend? Is that what this is about? It's as dumb as that?' He shrugs, embarrassed. 'Well, Saddam stood up to the Americans, didn't he?' And is that the only reason? He shrugs again. 'We hated Saddam Hussein. Like everyone else. We despised him. We couldn't stand him. But then he stood up to the Americans.'

'But he didn't believe anything you believe.'

They bring the coffee. Who's the idiot here? Them or me? I think of myself as less naive than Cherie Blair. But am I? Really? At least now I know why the wall's gone up. The Israelis want to separate themselves from people who display posters of Saddam Hussein. Who can blame them? Or – hold on, the old conundrum – do they display posters of Saddam Hussein because somebody just put up a wall?

Now we're driving back. We come to the checkpoint. The Israeli soldier is predictably furious. 'How did you get in? You're not allowed in. You know you're not allowed in.' Us smug, as if it were all *Dixon of Dock Green* and 'Sorry, officer.' Big grins. 'We found a way in.' But actually that's the point, isn't it? We found a way in. That's the point the Israelis don't want to understand. Even Professor Neill Lochery of London University, a friend of Israel, the author, for goodness' sake, of *Why Blame Israel?* has described the security fence as a white elephant. 'Already,' he says, 'the wall belongs to a bygone era.' Because before it was even finished, before the two billion had even been spent, Israel's enemies had switched tactics. They had abandoned suicide bombing, and moved on to missiles, to firing Qatam rockets, which sail oblivious way up high above the wall, fuelled by nothing but sugar and potassium nitrate. Future fights, says Lochery, will be in the sky. In other words, build a block, people go round it, or in this case over it. In the kernel of an idea lies that idea's incipient obsolescence.

No single move traps the king.

It's a nice road. We're going back on what's called the VIP road, because zooming away with white faces and two British passports we've been mistaken for settlers. So we have priority. We have a lovely empty road to ourselves. We can see the parallel road, the road for Palestinians, just fifty yards away, running alongside. Naturally, it's at a standstill. On that road the poor bastards have had to stop again at yet another of the six hundred and ninety-nine road blocks for what looks like most of the afternoon. But us? We sail through. My Palestinian friend lights a cigarette. 'Wherever you go, if you want to travel, there will be seventeen-year-old soldiers, Russians, Ethiopians, telling you how to live in your country. I'm old, so I put up with the humiliation, I absorb it.' He drags on his cigarette, his face shading now. 'But young people can't absorb it. They won't.'

Coming into Ramallah now. Raja Shehadeh, a lawyer who lives here, says that it is Ramallah's greatest good fortune not to be mentioned in the Bible. For that reason Ramallah is left alone, of no interest to fanatics, because its religious significance is precisely nothing. Nothing divine happened in Ramallah. What a stroke of luck for any town that wants to survive! Not to be named in any holy book! And along the cement wall, as we enter the town, are the blossoming graffiti. Oh yes, there's a parallel here and it's being made with aerosols and poster paints, so that every visitor will be forced to think 'Ah! Berlin!' The wall may be bygone for Professor Lochery, but for the inhabitants of the West Bank, it's all too real, blocking out the sun, blocking out the view, forbidding passage. There are people here on the West Bank who have not seen a body of water – lake nor sea – for fifteen years. The wittiest graffiti by far, in enormous capitals, the instruction scrawled across six cement blocks, just the letters:

CTL-ALT-DEL

as if at the press of three computer keys, the wall might disappear. Not a wall, just a drawing of a wall.

*

'We're fucked up, aren't we?' said a theatre friend of mine, on the phone from London. 'We're so fucked up. Have you ever known a time when people were so fucked up?' Then: 'A play about a wall. Fantastic! What a great idea. Because the wall is everything nowadays. We all live behind walls. Are you going to do a bit of Pyramus and Thisbe?' 'Do you know, as a matter of fact I'm not.'

'The wall is a symbol we cannot live together,' said my Israeli friend in the hotel in Tel Aviv. 'The wall tells the world we no longer wish to be normal. The project of being normal is over. It's an admission of failure.' And I wonder: If that's right, why would you want to look at failure all day? Why put up a wall to remind you, to draw attention to it? I mean, who in their right mind wants to make a metaphor concrete? You might as well dig a big pit in the middle of your country, light a fire at the bottom and call it hell.

'It's no fun fighting strangers,' says one Palestinian acquaintance. 'If you're going to fight, fight family. It's much more fun.' And it's true, Jews and Arabs are family; they remind you of each other, the children of Abraham, they remind each other of each other: same vitality, same wit, same land.

'You can tell a weak government by its eagerness to resort to strong measures,' said Benjamin Disraeli, Britain's only

Jewish prime minister. 'If we do not find the path to honest co-operation and honest negotiation with the Arabs, then we have learned nothing from over two thousand years of suffering and we deserve the fate that will befall us,' is what Albert Einstein said.

*

And now I'm sitting having tea in the Al-Kasaba cinema in Ramallah. It's the only working cinema on the West Bank. Mostly it shows Egyptian comedies. It's run by George Ibrahim, who's laughing, as he usually is. 'At the moment we are all enjoying jokes about the Western economy going to pieces because we can laugh and say 'It won't affect us because Palestine doesn't have an economy . . .' His friend, the playwright Salman Tamer, joins in. 'What is so shocking about Israel is that these days it doesn't even have a protest movement. In the old days, there were peaceniks on the streets and long-haired students. Now they have almost no anti-war movement at all. What can you say? A country which loses its hippies is in deep trouble.'

George drinks his tea and smiles. 'The wall is not around us. It's around them.'

And next day I'm in Jerusalem with David Grossman, the Israeli novelist whose son Yuri was killed on the last day of the Lebanon war. His house is still charged with grief. 'Of course at the foundation of the state there was a tremendous sense of purpose, of building something together. But we squandered our chance to make the state permanent in 1967. Instead of using the conquered territories as leverage in negotiation, instead we became addicted to occupation. When a people have suffered as much as we have it's not a bad feeling to be masters for once. And we became addicted to that feeling, like a narcotic.

'Now we have terrible trouble imagining any other reality than the one we live in. You become habituated, you cannot believe there is another possible way of life. And so effectively you become a victim of the situation. And here, again, is the central paradox, the idea of Israel was that we should cease to be victims. Instead we hand our fate over to the security people, we allow the army to run the country, because we lack a political class with a vision beyond the military. Survival becomes our only aim. We are living in order to survive, not in order to live.

'I want to begin to live. I want some gates in the wall.'